GW00371845

Abiotic The non-living factors that affect the type and number of organisms in a habitat. For example, weather, soil and type of landscape.

Absorption The step in digestion when absorbable molecules are passed into the blood and carried to all of the cells of the body.

Abundance The number of individuals in a population of a species in a habitat.

Acceleration When speed changes over time.

Acid A substance that turns blue litmus red. An acid solution has a pH less than 7.

Acid rain Rainwater with a pH of less than 5.5. The burning of fossil fuels releases gases into the air that dissolve in the air's moisture to form sulfuric acid and nitric acid. This falls back to Earth as acid rain.

Acquired characteristics Characteristics that are not inherited, but learned throughout life such as accent and being able to ride a bike.

Activation energy The minimum energy needed to start a chemical reaction.

Adaptation When an organism develops characteristics that make it better suited to its habitat.

Alkali A base that is soluble in water.

Alkali group

Alkal of the table.

Alloy A mixture of metals. For example, copper and tin are mixed to produce bronze.

Alternating current (a.c.) Electricity is generated in power stations in the form of alternating current. This means that the electrons in the wire are constantly changing direction every one-fiftieth of a second.

Alveoli Tiny air sacs in the lungs. This is where gases are exchanged between the air in lungs and dissolved gases in the blood.

Ammeter Measures the current flowing through a wire. Ammeters are connected in series.

Amniotic fluid Protective fluid that surrounds the embryo and foetus during pregnancy. Held within the amniotic sac.

Amplitude If you increase the amplitude of a sound wave, you increase its volume. An amplitude is the greatest displacement from its mean position, measured in metres (m).

Analogue An electrical signal that is created with many varying values.

Anther A part of the male structure (stamen) in flowering plants. The anther produces pollen which contains the male sperm. The anther also releases pollen grains.

Antibiotics A chemical produced by microorganisms that is used as a drug to treat certain diseases caused by bacteria and fungi.

Antimatter The mirror image of matter. Every particle of matter has a corresponding particle of antimatter. When they meet they destroy each other and are converted into pure energy.

Aorta The major artery in the body that leaves the left ventricle. It branches out into smaller arteries that deliver oxygenated blood to all cells of the body.

Apollo One of three spaceflight programmes created by NASA in response to President John F. Kennedy's desire to send a human to the Moon. The Apollo 11 mission in 1969 was the first time a human walked on the moon.

Archimedes' principle States that an object placed in water will feel an upthrust equal to the weight of the water it displaced.

Area The space taken up by a two-dimensional shape, such as a square or circle.

Artificial selection The breeding of plants and animals to improve their useful characteristics.

Asexual reproduction A form of reproduction that involves a single parent that produces offspring genetically identical to the parent.

Assimilation The step in digestion when the food is used by the body for energy and to build new cells.

Asteroid Lumps of rock that orbit the Sun but are too small to be classified as planets. There are three types of asteroids, divided based on what they are made up of: C-type asteroids are made up of carbon compounds; S-type asteroids are made up of stony material; M-type asteroids are mostly made of metals, such as iron.

Astronomy The area of science that looks at the universe and everything in it.

Atmosphere A mixture of gases that blanket the Earth's surface.

Atmospheric pressure The pressure exerted by the Earth's atmosphere. Atmospheric pressure affects weather.

Atom The smallest part of an element.

Atomic number The number of protons in the atom of that element.

Atomic structure The structure of the atom. It shows the location and the number of subatomic particles that make up an atom.

Atria (*singular: atrium*) The two upper chambers of the heart.

Average The typical number in a set of data.

Bacteria Single-cell organisms that do not have a nucleus.

Balance of nature Over time, the number and types of species in an ecosystem reach a steady state known as the balance of nature.

Balanced (*forces*) When an object does not move because competing forces cancel each other out, we say the forces are balanced.

Balanced diet A diet that provides carbohydrates, proteins, fats, vitamins, minerals, fibre and water in the correct quantities.

Base A substance that turns red litmus to blue. A basic solution has a pH greater than 7.

Battery Two or more cells stacked together.

Benign Benign tumours do not move to other parts of the body

Bias Bias is a strongly held personal opinion that may unfairly prejudge the outcome of a scientific investigation.

Big Bang Most scientists believe that the universe began with an explosion – the Big Bang – about 14 billion years ago.

Binary A binary number can only be made up of 1s and 0s. Computers use binary to store data.

Binary fission Bacteria divide by binary fission, meaning that one bacterial cell divides in two. The number of bacteria double with each generation.

Binomial nomenclature A system of naming living things. Each organism is identified by two names: the first identifying the genus of the organism and the second identifying the species. Both names are always in italics.

Biodegradable Materials that can be broken down by bacteria.

Biodiversity The great variety of life.

Biofuels Fuels created from plants; for example, biodiesel and bioethanol. These fuels can also be produced from other forms of biomass, including algae and faeces.

Biomass The quantity of matter in an organism.

Biome An ecosystem that extends over a very large area.

Biomolecules The key biomolecules needed by an organism are carbohydrates, proteins, fats and vitamins. Organisms use biomolecules as the building blocks of cells and as an energy source.

Bioremediation The use of microorganisms to break down harmful substances in damaged habitats.

Biosphere The part of Earth that can support life, made up of the crust and the atmosphere.

Biotechnology The use of living things or their parts of to make useful products and perform useful services. Biotechnology is important in industries such as medicine, farming and food science.

Biotic The living factors that affect the type and number of organisms in a habitat. For example, competition, predation and symbiosis.

Bit Each single number in binary (1 or 0) is known as a bit.

Body Mass Index A number calculated based on the height and weight of a person. It is often used as a tool to provide people with information about their weight and whether or not it is healthy.

Boiling A change of state from a liquid to a gas that involves all particles in the liquid.

Boiling point The temperature at which boiling and bubbling happens when a liquid changes state to a gas.

Bond Strong forces that chemically join together the elements in a compound.

Breaking reaction A reaction that releases stored energy to do cell work. For example, respiration.

Bud A small growth on a plant that can develop into a side branch, leaf or flower.

Building reaction A reaction that temporarily stores energy. For example, photosynthesis.

Bulb A short stem with fleshy leaves and buds. Excess food is stored in buds and forms a new bulb.

Buoyancy If the upthrust that results from the pressure of a liquid is large enough, it will keep an object afloat, or buoyant.

Burette A long narrow tube that is closed at the bottom with a tap. The acid is placed in the burette during a titration.

By-product The secondary product from the process of separating mixtures.

Byte Eight bits of information make up a byte.

Carbohydrates A biomolecule that is often an organism's preferred source of energy. Glucose, maltose, starch and cellulose are examples of carbohydrates.

Carbon cycle Explains how carbon is recycled through the Earth.

Carbon dioxide (CO_2) A greenhouse gas that is released into the atmosphere through respiration and the burning of fossil fuels (both carbon sources). CO_2 is needed for photosynthesis, which takes it out of the atmosphere (carbon sink).

Carbon footprint The total measure of greenhouse gas emissions caused by an organisation, event, product or individual.

Carbon sink Anything that takes carbon out of the atmosphere. For example, plants take carbon out of the atmosphere as carbon dioxide during photosynthesis.

Carbon source Anything that releases carbon into the atmosphere. For example, all living things release carbon into the atmosphere as carbon dioxide during respiration.

Carnivore Animals that eat animals only.

Carpel The female reproductive organs of flowering plants, made up of the stigma, style and ovary. The ovary contains the egg.

Catalyst A substance which speeds up the rate of a chemical reaction. At the end of the reaction it is chemically unchanged.

Celestial body Any natural body outside of the Earth's atmosphere. There are various celestial bodies, including planets, stars, moons, comets and asteroids.

Cell membrane A cell organelle that controls which materials move into and out of the cell.

Cell wall A plant cell organelle that is made up of cellulose. It makes the cell stronger.

Cells The building blocks of life. All organisms are made up of cells, either unicellular or multicellular.

Celsius (°C) One of the common scales used to measure temperature.

Cervix A part of the female reproductive system. The cervix is the narrow entrance to the uterus. It lets sperm enter the uterus on its way to the fallopian tube for fertilisation.

Chain reaction In nuclear fission, the splitting of a uranium isotope causes the release of more neutrons, which themselves can be used to cause further fission.

Characteristic A feature that helps identify a thing. For example, there are seven characteristics that identify living things: nutrition, respiration, excretion, growth, reproduction, movement and response.

Charged particles Particles that have lost or gained electrons.

Chemical

Chemical One of the forms in which energy can exist.

Chemical change A change that involves the formation of a new substance.

Chemical formula Shows the ratio of atoms of each element in the compound.

Chemical symbol Every element has its own chemical symbol, which appears in the periodic table of the elements. Most chemical symbols are based on the English name of the element, some are based on their Latin names and others are named after the scientists who discovered them.

Chlorination The step in water treatment where very small quantities of chlorine gases are added to the water to kill any harmful bacteria.

Chlorophyll A pigment in the chloroplasts of plant cells that allows the plant cell to absorb sunlight energy for photosynthesis.

Chloroplast A plant cell organelle that contains the pigment chlorophyll.

Chromatography Used to separate mixtures of substances in a solution. The different substances are carried up a piece of chromatography paper by the solvent at different rates.

Chromosomes Thread-like structures found in the nucleus of an animal or plant cell. They are made up of protein and DNA.

Circuit diagram An electronic circuit drawn using symbols.

Classification The system of grouping organisms together that share similar characteristics.

Climate change Long-term changes in the Earth's weather patterns. Commonly known as global warming.

Cloning Offspring that are genetically identical to each other and to the parent. These offspring are called clones.

Coefficient The numbers in front of chemical formulas. They indicate the number of molecules or ions of each kind involved in the reaction.

Collision theory Before a chemical reaction happens, the particles in the reactants must collide with each other. In order for the particles to react, the collision must have the correct amount of energy.

Combustion A fast oxidation reaction. When a substance burns it combines with oxygen in the air and gives out energy in the form of heat and light.

Comet A celestial body that orbits the Sun, made up of a nucleus, a coma and one or more tails. The nucleus of a comet is made up of dust and ice. The coma (a fuzzy outline or atmosphere caused by the Sun's radiation) is made up of carbon dioxide, dust and water vapour. The tail is made up of gas and dust produced by the nucleus.

Commercial space travel Journeys into space arranged by private companies with the goal of making a profit.

Communicate There are many ways to communicate scientific knowledge. These include public events, such as scientific demonstrations, research conferences, competitions or student science fairs; through the media, such as articles in newspapers, on the news, adverts on TV, science magazines and online; and by publication in scientific journals.

Community All of the different populations that live in a habitat.

Compass A small magnet allowed to move freely on a pivot. The direction the compass needle points is the direction of the magnetic field lines.

Competition The struggle between organisms for essential resources that are in short supply, such as food, space, oxygen, water, light and mates.

Components Objects in an electric circuit. The conversion of electrical energy into other forms takes place when that energy passes through these objects.

Composting A way of managing waste. Organic material is broken down by decomposers to reduce the volume of waste and return nutrients to the soil.

Compound Substances made up of two or more different elements chemically joined together by bonds.

Compress When a material is compressed, the material's particles move closer together.

Concave Concave lenses diverge light away from a point.

Concentrated solutions Contain a large quantity of solute in a small quantity of solvent.

Concentration The amount of solute in a given volume of solvent.

Condensation The change of state from a gas to a liquid. Cooling a gas takes energy from its particles so they slow down and move closer together to form a liquid.

Conduction The process through which solids transfer heat. When heat energy is transferred to a solid, it causes the particles of the solid to vibrate quickly. These vibrations pass through the rest of the solid, conducting the heat.

Conductor A substance that allows energy, such as heat or electricity, to pass through it easily.

Cones Cells in the retina of the eye that allow us to see colours.

Conical flask A flask designed so that the liquid can be swirled and mixed during a titration.

Conservation The careful management of the Earth's natural resources to prevent species from becoming extinct.

Consumers Organisms that must eat food (other organisms) as they cannot make their own food.

Contact forces Two objects have to be in contact for these forces to occur.

Contraception The deliberate prevention of fertilisation or implantation.

Contraction Contraction of a material means that it takes up a smaller volume of space.

Control A copy of an investigation, where every factor is the same except the variable under investigation (independent variable). Used for comparison.

Convection A process by which heat is transferred in liquids and gases.

Convection current When the particles of a liquid or gas are heated, they begin to rise. When they get to a certain point, they fall back down. If this process repeats itself, a convection current of moving particles is created.

Convex Convex lenses converge light on a point.

Core The centre of the Earth. The outer core is a thick liquid made up of molten iron and nickel. The inner core is also made up of iron and nickel, but here they are in a solid state because of the extremely high pressure.

Cornea The light is focused in the eye by a convex lens system made up of the cornea and the lens.

Corrosion The gradual weakening of metals by chemical reaction with their environment.

Covalent bond A bond formed when pairs of electrons are shared between two atoms. The shells containing the outer electrons overlap and this allows atoms to share electrons.

Cowper's gland Part of the male reproductive system. Produces fluids that nourish the sperm and allow them to swim. Together, these fluids and sperm make up semen.

Crest The highest point of a wave.

Crust The outside layer of the Earth is the crust. The oceans and continents lie on top of the crust.

Crystal lattice The regular repeating pattern of atoms in a crystal.

Crystallisation The formation of crystals by cooling a saturated solution.

Culturing The growth of large numbers of bacteria in a laboratory.

Cumulonimbus clouds The starting point for lightning. These clouds carry a positive charge on top and a negative charge below.

Current *(electricity)* The steady flow of charge though wires and circuits.

Cutting The most common type of vegetative propagation. Cuttings can be taken from the stem, root or leaf. If the cutting is placed in suitable conditions, a new plant will grow that is identical to the parent plant.

Cytoplasm A jelly-like substance surrounded by the cell membrane. Contains other organelles, including the nucleus, and dissolved substances such as oxygen.

Data Numbers or words that can be organised to give information.

Decibels The unit for measurement of sound intensity.

Decomposer An organism that breaks down dead plant or animal material. For example, bacteria, fungi and earthworms.

Decomposition Decomposition reactions break down a substance into simpler compounds or elements.

Defibrillator A device that sends a large voltage across the chest and heart muscle. This 'kick-starts' the heart into beating into a normal rhythm again.

Deficiency diseases Diseases caused by a lack of a particular nutrient. For example, anaemia is caused by a lack of iron in the diet.

Deforestation When large areas of forest are destroyed to make way for non-forest use, such as farmland, housing and roads.

Deform When forces compress or stretch objects, they deform them.

Density A measure of how much matter is in the object compared to how much space it takes up. It is the ratio of mass to volume.

Derived units Some physical quantities are measured in derived units. We calculate them by combining basic units in a specific way. For example, the unit for speed is metres per second (m/s). It is derived by dividing the basic unit of distance (metres) by the basic unit of time (seconds).

Desertification When land becomes more arid (dry) causing plants to die and become lost from a habitat.

Diaphragm A large sheet of muscle that plays a major role in breathing.

Diffusion Movement of particles from an area where they are high in concentration to an area where they are low in concentration.

Digestion

Digestion A stage in human nutrition. Large biomolecules in food are broken down into simpler, absorbable molecules. Takes place in the mouth, stomach and small intestine.

Digital A series of pulses known as binary (1 and 0).

Dilute solution Contains a small quantity of solute in a large quantity of solvent.

Diode A device that allows electric current to flow in one direction only. Used to convert a.c. to d.c.

Direct current (d.c.) Current that flows in one direction only.

Discharge The emission or release of electricity.

Disease A condition that affects an organism's ability to work normally. Diseases may have a number of causes, including certain microorganisms, abnormal genes and poor lifestyle choices.

Dispersion The splitting of white light into its seven colours.

Displacement Distance in a given direction. For example, 50 m north east. It is also the shortest distance between two points.

Dissipated Non-useful energy transfers, such as the heat emitted by a light bulb. When this happens, we say that the energy is dissipated in the form of heat.

Distance The length of the space between one point and another.

Distance–time graph Shows the distance something travels over the time taken to travel that distance. It is normally drawn by plotting the distance travelled on the y-axis and the time taken for the journey on the x-axis.

Distillation Used to separate a liquid and a soluble solid when you want to retain the solvent (liquid) or when separating two miscible liquids (liquids that mix together). Distillation separates miscible liquids based on their boiling points.

Distribution (habitat survey) The area(s) in a habitat where a species is located.

Division of labour The separate jobs carried out by the different parts of an organism.

DNA (deoxyribonucleic acid) The chemical found in genes that codes for all structures and processes in living organisms. It also plays a key role in inheritance and evolution.

Dominant When one gene for a trait is dominant over the other gene for that same trait, the dominant gene is the one that will show.

Drag forces Forms of friction, such as water resistance and air resistance.

Ductile Ductile metals can be drawn out to form a wire.

Dye-sensitised material A component of modern solar cells.

Dynamic equilibrium When an object has balanced forces acting upon it when it is moving.

Earthing When electricity travels through an object into the ground.

Eclipse When the light of the Sun is blocked by either the Moon or the Earth.

Ecology The study of how living things interact with their environment and each other.

Ecosystem A group of organisms interacting with each other and their environment.

Effervescence Bubbles of gas being produced by a chemical reaction.

Efficiency To measure how close we can get to the ideal of 100 per cent energy transfer in a device, we can calculate its efficiency.

Egestion A stage in human nutrition. Egestion is the release of undigested food from the body though the anus.

Egg The female gamete in both plants and animals.

Elastic Any object that is able to restore its shape after it has been extended or compressed is known as an elastic object.

Elastic limit The point at which an elastic object will not restore its shape.

Electrical *(energy)* Energy due to the presence of an electric field. This can be converted into other forms of energy.

Electrode A rod that dips into an electrolyte and completes the electrical circuit. There is a positive and negative electrode.

Electrolysis Splitting up a compound by passing electricity through it.

Electrolyte A substance that will conduct electricity when molten or dissolved in water.

Electromagnetic spectrum A band of waves with different energies, all of which travel at the speed of light.

Electromagnets A loop of wire wound around an iron core. Electromagnets can be turned on and off.

Electron One of the three subatomic particles that make up the atom. Electrons are found moving very quickly around the nucleus of the atom. They have a negative charge. Electrons are involved in the flow of electric charge through metals.

Electron beam A directed release of electrons.

Electronic mass balance

Electronic mass balance A device used to calculate the mass of an object.

Electronic configuration The location of electrons in an atom.

Element A substance made up of only one type of atom. An element cannot be split into simpler substances.

Embryo *(human)* Following fertilisation, the zygote divides to produce a ball of identical cells called an embryo.

Embryo *(plant)* Following fertilisation in flowering plants, the zygote divides and develops into an embryo.

Endoscope A device made of a number of wires of flexible glass known as optical fibres. Used to examine the inside of the body.

Endothermic A chemical reaction that absorbs heat energy from the surroundings. It involves a decrease in temperature.

Energy crisis A shortage in energy supply. A growing global population and new technology mean that the world's energy demands have increased.

Energy profile diagram Used to show energy transfers in chemical reactions. These diagrams show the energy stored in the reactants compared with the energy stored in the products.

Energy rating All modern homes for sale or rent in Ireland come with a Building Energy Rating (BER) Certificate. The BER is the calculated energy use for space and hot water heating, ventilation and lighting of the home. The scale of the BER goes from A to G, with A being the most efficient rating.

Energy transfer diagram A way of representing the useful energy transfers that can take place in a device or process.

Enrichment Fertilisers may contain toxic chemicals that can poison organisms. If too much fertiliser is spread, nutrients can be washed off the soil and into nearby rivers and lakes, which often results in a 'bloom' of algae and a loss of oxygen from the water.

Enzyme Often called biological catalysts, as they control the rate of and organise all of the chemical reactions within a cell. Each enzyme controls a step in a chemical reaction. Examples of enzymes include amylase, maltase and catalase.

Epididymis A coiled tube on the outside of the testis that stores sperm.

Equilibrium An object is in equilibrium when it is subject to balanced forces.

Error If data is measured in the correct way, it is inaccurate data.

When this happens, it is known as an error in the measurement.

Ethics The need to carry out investigations and produce findings in a responsible way.

Evaluate Evaluating an investigation involves commenting on how the findings relate to the original hypothesis and on the investigation's strengths and weaknesses.

Evaporation A change of state from a liquid to a gas. The particles with the most energy leave the surface, spread out and form a gas. The liquid does not bubble and evaporation happens at all temperatures.

Evolution The gradual change in the inherited characteristics of a population over time. Evolution can lead to new species.

Excretion The removal of waste from cells.

Exhalation The act of breathing out.

Exosphere The uppermost layer of the Earth's atmosphere, where it merges with space.

Exothermic A chemical reaction that produces heat. Heat energy is transferred from the chemicals to the surroundings. It involves an increase in temperature.

Expansion Expansion of an object occurs when it takes up a greater volume of space.

Extinct An animal or plant is extinct when there are no more individuals of the species alive anywhere in the world.

Fair To keep a test fair, you must identify the independent, dependent and controlled (fixed) variables.

Fallopian tube A part of the female reproductive system. The funnel-shaped opening of the fallopian tube captures the egg released at ovulation. Fertilisation usually takes place in the fallopian tube.

Fats A biomolecule that stores energy. Fats also play a role in protection and insulation.

Feeding relationship The way energy and nutrients are passed from one organism to another.

Fertilisation The step in reproduction when the egg and sperm fuse together to form a zygote.

Filament A part of the male structure (stamen) in flowering plants. The filament is a stalk that positions the anther so the pollen can be blown away by the wind or picked up by an insect.

Filter A device that can be placed in front of white light to absorb all colours except its own. For example, a blue filter will allow blue light to pass through it and absorb all other colours.

Filtration

Filtration *(separation technique)* Used to separate insoluble solids from liquids. Filtration works because small particles (the water) can pass through holes in the filter paper. The insoluble solid (the sand) stays in the filter paper.

Filtration *(water treatment)* The step in water treatment when the water passes through beds of sand and gravel. Any remaining particles are removed.

Fire triangle Three conditions are needed to make a fire happen: fuel, heat and oxygen. If any part of the fire triangle is removed, the fire will extinguish.

Fission The splitting of an isotope of the element uranium into two smaller nuclei with the release of neutrons and energy.

Flexible films Devices used to make modern solar cells.

Flower The part of the plant responsible for sexual reproduction. It contains the male and female sex organs.

Fluoridation The final step in water treatment where flourine is added to prevent tooth decay and the pH of the water is checked to make sure it is within an acceptable range (pH 7–8).

Flyby Space missions that involve sending a craft past a planet or other body, taking pictures on its way to another destination. These craft are known as probes.

Foetus By the end of the eight week of pregnancy, the embryo is approximately 3 cm long. From this point, the embryo is called a foetus.

Food chain Describes a feeding relationship using arrows to show which organisms eat others.

Food pyramid A tool to promote healthy eating and to help people plan a balanced diet. The general rule is that you eat the most servings from the base of the pyramid and only small quantities from the top.

Food web Made up of interconnected food chains. Feeding relationships are better shown using a food web as organisms usually feed on many different food sources and may also be eaten by more than one consumer.

Force Forces explain why an object moves the way it does, why things stretch, twist, tear, snap, bend, break, speed up, slow down and change shape. Pushes and pulls are types of force.

Force field A region in space where an object feels a force.

Force meter Used to measure forces digitally.

Forward biased When the positive end of the diode is connected to the positive end of the battery. This allows current to flow.

Fossil fuels Fuels formed from the remains of dead plants and animals. Coal, oil, peat and natural gas are examples of fossil fuels.

Fracking Also known as hydraulic fracturing. A technique that has been developed to help extract natural gas from rocks. Fracking involves drilling down into the earth and injecting a mixture of water, sand and chemicals into the rock at high pressure, which releases the gas trapped inside the rock.

Fractional distillation How crude oil is separated. The crude oil is heated and turns into a gas. The gas is put into a large tower and cools as it rises up the tower. Substances with high boiling points turn to liquid at the bottom of the tower and substances with low boiling points turn to liquid at the top.

Freezing A change of state from a liquid to a solid. Cooling a liquid takes energy from its particles so they can only vibrate, not move around. The liquid freezes into a solid.

Frequency *(habitat survey)* The percentage chance of a particular species being present in a randomly chosen quadrat.

Frequency *(sound)* How fast a sound wave is moving. The faster the sound wave moves, the higher pitch it will have.

Friction A force that opposes motion when two objects are placed in contact.

Fruit Following fertilisation in flowering plants, the ovary develops into the fruit, which helps to protect and disperse the seed.

Fuel A substance that burns in oxygen to produce heat.

Fungi One of the five kingdoms of organisms. Fungi can be unicellular or made up of long threads. Fungi are decomposers. Fungi cannot make their own food by photosynthesis.

Fuse A safety measure used to prevent electric shocks. The fuse has a thin piece of wire running through it, designed to melt if the current goes above a set value. When the fuse wire melts, it breaks the circuit cutting off the electricity.

Fusion When two smaller nuclei combine into a large nucleus with the release of large amounts of energy.

Galaxy A large group of stars, dust, gas and dark matter held together by gravity.

Gametes Sex cells. The male gamete is a sperm and the female gamete is an egg.

Gas

Gas There is a lot of space between particles in a gas. The particles move about to fill the container that they are in.

Gas giants The outer planets in our solar system are called gas giants because they are mainly made of gases hydrogen and helium.

Gas pressure As gas particles move around, they collide with other objects and with each other. This force, applied over an area, causes gas pressure. The faster the gas particles move, the more force they exert, so the greater the pressure is.

Gene A short section of DNA. Each gene codes for a different protein in a cell.

Genetic cross Used to study the inheritance of characteristics or traits (controlled by genes) from parents to offspring.

Genetic engineering Deliberately changing genes to produce desirable characteristics.

Genetics The study of how characteristics are passed on from one generation to another.

Geocentric A theory of the structure of the solar system in which the Earth was thought to be at the centre.

Geothermal Heat energy from the Earth. A geothermal power station draws heat from the Earth's core to heat steam and turn turbines

Geotropism The growth of a plant in response to the force of gravity.

Germination The growth of a seed to form a new plant. The final stage of sexual reproduction in flowering plants.

Global warming An increase in the temperature of the Earth's atmosphere that causes climate change.

Glucose A type of carbohydrate. Plants produce glucose as a result of photosynthesis. Glucose is the preferred source of energy for respiration for the majority of organisms.

Graduated cylinder A piece of equipment used to measure the volume of a liquid.

Grafting A type of vegetative propagation. Grafting involves joining a bud or stem of a valuable plant to a plant that already has a well-developed root system. Grafting is most commonly used to grow new fruit trees that produce high-quality fruit.

Graphene Carbon broken down into a sheet that is one atom thick. This material is extremely strong, ultra-thin and can conduct large electric currents.

Gravity A non-contact force of attraction between objects. There is a gravitational pull between all masses.

Greenhouse effect Greenhouse gases act like a blanket, trapping heat from the Sun near the Earth's surface. This causes the Earth to become warmer.

Greenhouse gases Gases such as carbon dioxide and methane that act like a blanket, trapping heat near the Earth's surface.

Groups There are eight groups in the periodic table. A group is a vertical column of elements. All the elements in a group have similar properties.

Growth An increase in the size (biomass) of an organism.

Habitat The place where an organism lives and to which it is best adapted.

Haemoglobin A biomolecule that contains iron and picks up oxygen for transport. The cytoplasm of red blood cells is rich in haemoglobin.

Heat *(energy)* A form of energy that is generated by the movement of atoms and molecules. Heat is released by organisms during respiration.

Heliocentric A theory of the structure of the solar system where the Sun is at the centre.

Herbivore Organisms that eat plants only.

Homeostasis Organisms must ensure that conditions stay the same, even though its environment may change. This quest for 'sameness' is called homeostasis.

Human population The number of humans living on Earth.

Human missions Space missions that involve landing on an object to study it carefully. These missions carry the greatest risk to human life. The Moon landings were the last human missions to land on another celestial body.

Hydrocarbon A compound made of hydrogen and carbon.

Hydrochloric acid Carbon dioxide gas can be prepared in the school laboratory by reacting an acid, such as hydrochloric acid, with a carbonate, such as calcium carbonate.

Hydroelectric *(energy)* An energy source that uses the kinetic energy of falling water to turn turbines and generate electricity.

Hydrogen A gas that can be used as a source of energy.

Hydrogen peroxide Oxygen is prepared in the laboratory by breaking the chemical bonds in hydrogen peroxide molecules. Hydrogen peroxide will break into water and oxygen gas.

Hypothesis An idea, drawing on previous knowledge, that will be tested by an investigation.

Identification key Used to identify an unknown animal or plant during a habitat study.

Igneous Rocks that are produced when magma breaks through the surface of the Earth's crust during a volcano and cools. Granite and basalt are examples of igneous rock.

Implantation The embedding of the embryo into the wall of the uterus (womb).

Impure substance Also known as a mixture. A material containing two or more elements or compounds that are in close contact and are mixed.

Incineration The burning of waste. It quickly reduces the volume of waste that is sent to landfill sites. However, the burning of materials releases poisonous gases into the air.

Indicator A substance that shows whether a solution being tested is an acid or a base. Indicators contain a dye that turns a different colour in acidic or alkaline solutions.

Information age A time in which people have access to a large amount of digital information.

Infrared Heat is radiated in the form of infrared waves. This is how heat transfers from the Sun to the Earth. Hot bodies radiate infrared – the hotter the body, the greater the amount of infrared it radiates.

Ingestion A stage in human nutrition. The act of eating food.

Inhalation The act of breathing in.

Inherited characteristics Characteristics passed on from parents to their children by genes. For example, hair colour and blood type.

Insoluble Solids that do not dissolve are called insoluble.

Insulator A substance that does not allow energy, such as heat or electricity, to pass through it easily.

Interaction pair Pairs of forces that occur together.

Intercostal muscles Muscles located between the ribs that are used in inhalation and exhalation.

Interdependence When two organisms depend on each other for an important aspect of their survival.

International Space Station (ISS) A research facility that orbits Earth, where astronauts can investigate the impact of weightlessness on different living things. The ISS is in low orbit and completes one orbit of the Earth every 90 minutes. Because of this, it is important in the observation of global weather systems.

Invertebrates Animals that do not have a backbone.

Ion When an atom loses or gains an electron, it becomes an ion. An ion is a charged atom.

Ionic bond When metals and non-metals react they form an ionic bond. This is a force of attraction between oppositely charged ions in a compound. It is a bond that involves the giving and receiving of electrons from one atom to another atom.

Iris Part of the eye. Controls the size of the pupil.

Isotope Atoms with the same number of protons but different numbers of neutrons are called isotopes.

Kilocalories (kcal) A unit measuring the energy content of food. 1 kcal is equal to 4.2 kJ.

Kilojoules (kJ) A unit for measuring the energy content of food. As the joule is a small quantity of energy, the energy content of foodstuffs are more commonly described in thousands of joules, as kilojoules.

Kilowatt-hour (kWh) The SI unit of electricity.

Kinetic Relating to motion. Any moving object has kinetic energy.

Kingdoms Organisms are classified into five broad groups, or kingdoms: animals, plants, protists, fungi and bacteria.

Lactation The production of breast milk.

Landfill A method of waste management. Waste is buried in the ground and left to decompose over an extended period of time.

Large Hadron Collider (LHC) One of the most advanced particle accelerators in existence, located at CERN in Geneva, Switzerland. It uses high-energy electric fields to accelerate particles close to the speed of light around a circular loop. When these particles collide, their kinetic energy is converted into matter that can be studied.

Law Any theory that has been tested by many different scientists over a long period of time and is yet to be proven false.

Law of conservation of energy States that energy cannot be created or destroyed, but can only be changed from one form to another.

Law of conservation of mass States that matter cannot be created or destroyed but can change from one form to another. In a chemical reaction, the total mass of all the reactants always equals the total mass of the products.

Leaf A plant organ made up of the blade, veins and stalk. Its roles include photosynthesis, food storage, exchange of gases, water transport, asexual reproduction and protection of the plant.

Length *(versus resistance)* The longer a component in a circuit is, the harder it is for charges to get from one side to the other and so the greater the resistance.

Lens *(eye)* The light is focused in the eye by a convex lens system consisting of the cornea and the lens.

Lens *(microscope)* A part of the light microscope that is responsible for focusing light and magnifying the image of specimens. There are two types of lens in a light microscope: eyepiece and objective.

Lenticel Loosely packed areas of bark or tissue, through which woody plants and some fruits exchange gases with the atmosphere.

Light *(energy)* A form of energy.

Light-emitting diode A diode that emits light when current flows through it.

Light microscope An instrument used to view magnified images of small specimens, such as plant and animal cells, clearly.

Lightning A visible effect of static electricity. Cumulonimbus clouds carry a positive charge on top and a negative charge below. The negative charge in the cloud induces a positive charge on the Earth and the two opposite charges try to connect. The energy built up between the cloud and the ground causes a discharge of giant sparks.

Lightning conductors Metal rods placed on the top of tall buildings and connected to a metal plate in the ground. They are used to draw lightning from clouds safely to the ground.

Light telescope An instrument that uses visible light to produce magnified images of distant objects.

Light-year The distance that light travels in one year. Light-years are often used in astronomy to describe the distance to faraway stars and galaxies.

Line transect A way of investigating the distribution of a plant species across a habitat. A rope is laid out across the habitat and marked with a knot at every metre. Each knot is checked to see if the species under survey has touched the line transect and the result is recorded.

Liquid When a material is in the liquid state the particles are very close together. Most particles touch each other. The particles in a liquid have more energy than the particles in a solid. This means that the particles can move around and slide past each other so a liquid can flow and change its shape.

Litmus indicator Changes colour from blue to red in acids and from red to blue in alkalis. Litmus does not indicate how concentrated the acid or alkali is.

Littering A form of pollution. The careless disposal of waste.

Live The live wire in a house circuit is high in electrical potential energy.

Loudness A property of sound waves. Loudness is affected by amplitude.

Lubrication Friction between solids can be reduced by using lubrication. Examples of lubricants include oil and wax.

Luminous A luminous object transforms and emits its own light, such as stars, a light bulb or a candle.

Lunar eclipse Happens when the Earth's shadow falls on the Moon.

Lunar phases The shape of the illuminated part of the Moon as seen on Earth. They repeat over a period of time, which allows us to predict the type of Moon we will see at any given time.

Lungs Two large, spongy, elastic organs located in the chest cavity. They expand during inhalation and shrink during exhalation.

Magma A mixture of hot molten or semi-molten rock underneath the Earth's mantle.

Magnetic (energy) Energy due to the presence of a magnetic field. This can be converted into other forms of energy.

Magnetic field The space around a magnet that exerts a force on magnets and magnetic materials.

Magnetic field lines The directions of forces in a magnetic field are represented by magnetic field lines.

Magnetic materials Materials magnets attract. For example, iron, steel, cobalt and nickel, as well as other magnets.

Magnetic resonance imaging (MRI) Scanning devices that use a very strong magnetic field, generated by electromagnets, to create an image of the inside of the body.

Magnetism A physical phenomenon arising from the force caused by magnets.

Magnets Pieces of metal that attract other substances.

Malignant Malignant tumours can spread through the body and are a more serious medical concern than benign tumours.

Malleable A material that can be hammered into various shapes without cracking.

Malnutrition Malnutrition refers to a diet that is not balanced and negatively affects a person's health.

Manganese dioxide One of the catalysts that can be used to speed up the breaking of chemical bonds in hydrogen peroxide molecules.

Mantle Beneath the Earth's crust is the mantle. It is mostly made up of solid rock, except for the upper mantle, which is made of magma.

Marble chips The common name for calcium carbonate.

Mass A measure of the amount of matter in an object.

Mass number The total sum of the protons plus neutrons in the nucleus of an atom.

Matter Any substance that takes up space and has a mass.

Measuring Assessing the value of something using appropriate instruments.

Medium A material that light can pass through, such as air, water, plastic or diamond.

Melting A change of state from a solid to a liquid. When solids are heated their particles gain energy and move apart. The particles break free from the fixed positions they were in and the solid changes to a liquid.

Melting point The temperature at which a substance melts.

Meniscus In a graduated cylinder, the surface of the liquid does not appear to be level, with the centre point of the liquid appearing to be lower than the edges touching the cylinder. This bowl shape is known as a meniscus.

Menopause A phase that signals the end of a female's ability to reproduce and also the end of her menstrual cycle.

Menstrual cycle The repeating series of changes that take place in the female body to prepare it for pregnancy. The cycle can range from 21 to 40 days. A typical menstrual cycle is 28 days.

Mesosphere A layer of the Earth's atmosphere. The mesosphere ranges from 50 to 80 km above the Earth's surface.

Metabolism All of the chemical reactions that take place in the cells of organisms.

Metamorphic Rocks formed when igneous and sedimentary rocks are changed into harder rocks by high temperatures and pressure. Examples of metamorphic rocks include quartzite, slate and marble.

Meteorologist A scientist who studies the Earth's atmosphere to predict the weather.

Metre stick A piece of equipment that can be used to measure the length of a straight line.

Metric system A common system of measuring physical quantities where units are based on multiples of ten.

Micrograph An image formed by an electron microscope.

Micrometer A device used to measure the width, length and thickness of small objects.

Microorganisms Very small organisms. They cannot be seen by the human eye alone and must be viewed under microscopes. For example, bacteria and viruses.

Micropropagation A type of vegetative propagation. A small sample of tissue is taken from the root, stem, leaf or bud of the parent plant.

Microwaves Electromagnetic waves that are higher in energy than radio waves. Wi-Fi and Bluetooth signals are transmitted using microwaves.

Minerals Substances that organisms need in small amounts to build biomolecules and to assist chemical reactions within cells.

Mitochondria Tiny organelles in the cytoplasm of cells. Respiration reactions take place in the mitochondria.

Mixture A material containing two or more elements or compounds that are in close contact and are mixed. The parts that make up a mixture are not chemically combined. Mixtures can usually be easily separated into its parts.

Model A representation of a process or idea in a simpler way, making it easy to understand.

Molecule A group of two or more atoms bonded together.

Moon A natural satellite that orbits a planet.

Movement All organisms move. Animals move all of their parts to find food, mates and shelter or to escape danger. Plants move parts of themselves to access sunlight, water and so on.

Multicellular Organisms made up of more than one cell. Complex multicellular organisms, such as humans, are often made up of billions of cells.

Mutagen Any environmental factor that increases the likelihood of mutation.

Mutation A change in a gene or chromosome. Mutation can be inherited or influenced by an organism's environment.

Nanotechnology The science of the very small. The nanoscale accounts for anything that is smaller than 1 nanometre (1×10^{-9} metres).

NASA The National Aeronautics and Space Administration. A government body in the USA that works to advance humankind in the areas of aeronautics, human exploration, science and space technology.

Natural selection The process by which the members of a species who are best suited to their environment are most likely to survive and reproduce.

Negative Electrons have a negative charge. If an object gains electrons, it becomes negatively charged.

Neutral *(pH)* Substances that do not behave like acids or bases. Their pH is exactly 7.

Neutral *(wire)* The neutral wire in a house circuit is low in electrical potential energy.

Neutralisation Neutralisation reactions are reactions between acids and bases to form salt and water.

Neutron A neutral subatomic particle found in the centre of an atom. A neutron has a neutral charge.

Newton meter A device used to measure forces. Also known as a spring balance.

Niche The role of an organism in a habitat, including what it eats, what it is eaten by, whom it mates with and how it interacts with the non-living environment.

Nitrogen cycle Explains how nitrogen is recycled through the Earth.

Non-contact forces Forces where objects do not have to be in contact for the forces to occur.

Non-luminous Non-luminous objects reflect light from other sources. You can read the words on this page because light from another source is reflecting off the book and entering into your eyes.

Non-renewable *(materials)* Materials that will not renew themselves at a rate quick enough to meet demand.

Nuclear *(energy)* A form of energy released by a nuclear reaction (fusion or fission).

Nuclear power Power that is generated when nuclear fission converts nuclear energy into heat energy.

Nuclear reactor A nuclear reactor uses the heat energy produced by nuclear fission to generate steam and turn turbines.

Nucleus *(atom)* The middle of an atom, where protons and electrons are located.

Nucleus *(cell)* The organelle that controls the activities of the cell. Genes are found in the nucleus.

Nutrient cycle The cycling of matter and minerals through the living and non-living parts of the Earth.

Nutrition How organisms get their food.

Obesity If an organism consumes more energy than the body requires, then this excess energy will be converted to fat. In extreme cases this may lead to obesity, which is linked to an increased likelihood of diseases such as type 2 diabetes, stroke and heart disease.

Ohmmeter Resistance can be measured with an ohmmeter connected in series.

Ohms (Ω) Electrical resistance is measured in ohms.

Omnivore Animals that eat both plants and animals.

Opaque A material that allows no light to pass through and forms a shadow. For example, a table, chair or a human.

Opisometer A device that can be used to measure the length of short curved lines.

Optical fibres Wires of flexible glass that are used to transmit light signals. They are used in devices such as endoscopes and high-speed internet cables.

Optic nerve Carries impulses from the retina to the brain.

Orbiter A spacecraft or satellite that circles around a planet or moon to take detailed measurements of that body and help inform future landing missions on these bodies.

Organ A group of tissues that work together to perform a task that an individual tissue could not carry out on its own.

Organelles Structures within cells that are produced from biomolecules. Each organelle performs a particular task.

Organisation All living organisms are composed of cells. Cooperation amongst cells forms tissues; cooperation amongst tissues forms organs, and so on. All of this cooperation is called organisation.

Organism All living things. Every organism demonstrates the seven characteristics of life.

Outlier Typically, random errors cause specific readings to be either too high or too low. When compared with the rest of the readings taken, these readings will stand out as outliers.

Ovaries *(human)* A part of the female reproductive system. A female has two ovaries. On average, the ovaries produce an egg every 28 days (ovulation). The ovaries also produce important hormones, including oestrogen and progesterone.

Ovary (plant) Located in the carpel of flowering plants. The ovary produces the egg and after fertilisation and may develop into a fruit.

Overflow can A can with an angled spout that can be used to find the volume of large, irregular-shaped solids.

Ovulation The release of an egg from the ovary.

Oxidation Oxidation reactions take place when a substance reacts with oxygen. For example, combustion reactions and corrosion (rusting) of metals.

Oxygen (O_2) A key gas in the atmosphere. Oxygen is produced as a waste product of photosynthesis. Oxygen is needed for respiration, and is therefore the most efficient release of energy from food. Oxygen is also needed for combustion.

Ozone (O_3) A compound of oxygen. Ozone is present in the upper atmosphere (stratosphere). It is crucial to life on Earth as it absorbs a lot of the Sun's potentially harmful UV light.

Parallel When components in an electrical circuit have multiple connections coming from a point, they are connected in parallel.

Parasite An organism that lives on or in another living thing.

Particle A tiny individual piece of a substance.

Particle accelerator A device that uses electric force fields to accelerate charged particles to very high speeds. These particles are then collided with surfaces or with each other, converting their kinetic energy into different forms.

Particle size Used to compare the dimensions of particles in solids.

Particle theory Scientists still believe that everything is made from very small particles. This idea is used to explain the properties of solids, liquids and gases.

Pathogen Any organism that causes disease.

Peer review When a scientific article is judged by other scientists to see if it is scientifically valid.

Penis A part of the male reproductive system. The penis transfers semen to the vagina of the female during ejaculation.

Penumbra One of the two types of shadows observed during an eclipse. A penumbra occurs when the light source is only partially blocked and there is only a partial shadow.

Percentage cover The proportion of ground covered by plants or animals. Percentage cover may be calculated during a quantitative survey of a habitat.

Periodic table A list of all known elements arranged in groups to show patterns in their properties.

Periods The horizontal rows of elements across the periodic table. The period number also tells us the number of shells an atom has.

Phloem Tissue that transports food around a plant.

pH meter A digital method of measuring pH that indicates very small differences in pH.

Photosynthesis The way plants convert energy from the Sun into chemical energy to make their own food, using carbon dioxide and water from their environment.

Phototropism The growth of a plant toward light.

pH scale A scale that is used to show how concentrated an acid or alkali is. A substance that has a pH of 7 on the pH scale is neutral. A substance that has a pH below 7 is acidic. A substance that has a pH above 7 is alkaline. The extremes of the pH scale are the most concentrated and most dangerous acids and bases.

Physical change A change in which no new substance is formed. There is no change in mass and the reaction can be easily reversed.

Physical quantity A quantity that can be measured.

Pipette A glass tube designed to deliver an exact volume of solution.

Pitch The frequency of a sound determines its pitch. Sounds with a high frequency have a high pitch and sounds with a low frequency have a low pitch.

Placenta A temporary organ in the womb that allows materials to pass between the mother and the foetus during pregnancy.

Plane mirror Mirrors designed to achieve a high level of regular reflection.

Planet An object that is in orbit around a star, has sufficient mass to assume a nearly round shape, and has become gravitationally dominant. This means that it can clear the space debris in its orbit.

Plasma The liquid part of blood. It is made up of 92 per cent water. A number of important substances are dissolved in plasma. It also carries blood cells.

Plate tectonics The movement of large chunks of the Earth's crust.

Plumule A shoot that emerges from the seed during germination and will develop into the plant shoot.

Poles (*Earth's magnetic field*) The spot on the Earth towards which a compass needle will point north. The magnetic north pole is in the region near the geographic South Pole and vice versa.

Poles *(magnets)* Two opposite ends of a magnet at which the magnetic field is at its strongest.

Pollination A stage in the sexual reproduction of flowering plants. Pollination takes place when the pollen travels from the anther of the male part of a flower to the style of the female part of a flower. Pollination can be carried out by wind, by insects or by other animals.

Pollution When harmful substances are added to the environment. There are three types of pollution: air, water and soil.

Polymerisation The step in plastics production when small repeating units called monomers bond together to form larger chains called polymers.

Population All of the individual organisms of the same species in a habitat.

Positive An object that has lost electrons takes on a positive charge.

Potential *(energy)* The energy an object has due to its shape or position. For example, an object can have potential kinetic energy due to its position against gravity. The higher up it goes, the more it goes against gravity and the more potential energy it gains.

Potential difference When there is a point of high electrical energy and a point of low electrical energy in a complete circuit, we say that there is a difference in electrical potential energy between those points. Provides the energy that pushes electrons around a circuit. It is needed to make a current flow.

Power A measure of how quickly a machine transfers energy from one form to another. In a more powerful object, energy is transferred at a faster rate.

Predation Controls the number of organisms in an ecosystem through the preying of some animals on others.

Predator An animal that hunts, kills and eats another animal (prey).

Pressure A measure of the force exerted per unit area of an object.

Prey An animal that is hunted, killed and eaten by another animal (predator).

Primary cell A cell that cannot be recharged once it is used up.

Primary colours Of the colours in the white light spectrum, red, green and blue are known as primary colours. Combining these three colours makes white light.

Principle A theory that has been subjected to testing by different scientists over a long time and is yet to be proven false. Another term for a law.

Prism Used to split white light into a spectrum of seven colours.

Producers Organisms that are able to make their own food. Plants, algae and certain bacteria use sunlight energy to make their food (photosynthesis).

Product A new substance formed in a chemical reaction.

Product life cycle All products go through similar steps during their production: 1. Extraction of raw materials; 2. Manufacturing; 3. Packaging and distribution; 4. Product use; 5. End-of-life disposal.

Properties The features and behaviour of a material.

Prostate gland Part of the male reproductive system. The seminal vesicles and prostate gland produce fluids that nourish the sperm and allow them to swim. Together, these fluids and sperm make up semen.

Proteins A biomolecule that organisms need for growth, repair and enzymes.

Protists One of the five kingdoms of organisms. There are many different kinds of protist. This kingdom includes plankton, algae, slime and water moulds.

Proton A positively charged subatomic particle found in the nucleus of an atom.

Puberty All humans are born sexually immature. At puberty, the reproductive organs develop and become sexually mature in response to changing hormone levels. Secondary sexual characteristics also develop at puberty.

Pulmonary artery The pulmonary artery leaves the right ventricle and delivers deoxygenated blood to lungs, where carbon dioxide is removed and oxygen is taken on board.

Pulse A wave of vibration that passes through an artery in response to blood being forced out of the left ventricle. The pulse can be felt at an artery close to surface of skin, such as in the wrist.

Pupil An opening that lets light into the eye.

Pure substance Contains only atoms or molecules of that substance.

Quadrat A square frame made of metal, plastic or wood that is used during quantitative surveys of habitats.

Qualitative data Data recorded using words. Also called categorical data.

Qualitative survey

Qualitative survey A list of the different species in a habitat.

Quantitative data Data recorded in numbers, also called numerical data.

Quantitative survey Numerical data about the species in a habitat.

Quantity An exact amount or number of things.

Radiation A process of heat transfer that does not involve the movement or vibration of particles.

Radicle The part of the plant embryo that will develop into the root system. During germination, the seed coat splits and the radicle grows out and downwards into soil.

Radioactive Radioactive materials release harmful radioactive particles and energy in the form of gamma rays as they decay.

Radio telescope An instrument that uses radio waves to produce visual images of distant objects.

Radio waves The lowest energy waves on the electromagnetic spectrum.

Random errors This type of error is caused by using a faulty technique when taking a measurement or by a difference in the reaction times of two people taking a measurement.

Range The difference between the lowest and highest values in a set of data.

Rate of reaction How quickly a chemical reaction happens.

Reactant A chemical that reacts with another chemical during a chemical reaction.

Reaction *(force)* The force applied by an object in response to another force.

Reactivity series of metals A guide developed by scientists to compare how easily various metals react with air, water and dilute acid.

Recessive When one gene for a trait is dominant over the recessive gene for that same trait, the recessive gene will not show. Instead, the dominant gene will show.

Recycling Reusing the materials an unwanted object is made from. Paper, glass, metal and plastic can all be recycled.

Reference Intakes (RI) Values that provide information about the amount of calories (energy), fat, sugars and salt needed for a healthy diet.

Reflection When light hits different surfaces, it bounces off those surfaces.

Refraction As light travels from one medium to another, it changes direction.

Reliable *(method)* A method that is reproducible and repeatable.

Renewable Renewable energy sources are sources that will not run out.

Repeatable *(method)* If you repeat an investigation several times, or if you repeat a measurement in an investigation, you should be able to collect and record similar data each time.

Reproducible *(method)* If somebody follows your method, they should be able to collect and record similar data to data that was collected in the original investigation.

Reproduction Being able to produce new individuals (offspring). Reproduction ensures that a species will not become extinct. There are two forms of reproduction: sexual and asexual.

Resistance A measure of how difficult it is for an electric charge to pass through something.

Resistor Any object or substance that opposes the flow of electric charge.

Respiration The release of energy from food.

Response Organisms must be able to sense and respond to changes in their environment.

Retina A layer of nerve cells at the back of the eye that sends impulses through the optic nerve to the brain.

Reverse biased When the negative end of the diode is connected to the positive end of the battery. No current flows.

Risk assessment Describes the potential hazards of an investigation, outlines the steps taken to reduce those hazards and identifies the person responsible for reducing those hazards.

Robotic lander Missions that involve landing a robotic spacecraft in a location that has been mapped out by an orbiter.

Rock cycle Rocks are changed by weathering, erosion, heat and pressure. The rock cycle describes how and why these changes take place.

Rods Cells found on the retina that allow us to see in black and white.

Root The part of the plant that grows in the soil. It anchors and supports the plant in the soil and absorbs water and minerals from the soil. Some roots can store food and water.

Ruler A piece of equipment that can be used to measure the length of straight lines.

Runner A new stem produced by the parent plant that grows across the surface of the ground. A bud at the tip of the runner produces a new root and shoot system. It is a form of asexual reproduction in certain plants.

Salt An acid and a base react to produce a salt and water in a neutralisation reaction. A salt is a chemical compound, formed when the hydrogen part of an acid is replaced by a metal. Examples of salts include sodium chloride, magnesium chloride and calcium chloride.

Sankey diagram A way of representing the useful and wasteful energy transfers that can take place in a device or process.

Saturated solution A solution that contains as much solute as possible at that temperature.

Scalar A physical quantity that has magnitude only. For example, time.

Scales A device that can be used to measure mass. For example, bathroom scales can be used to measure the mass of a person.

Scientific method How scientists investigate natural occurrences (phenomena). A scientist will propose a hypothesis, then set out to demonstrate that, at this point in time, their hypothesis is not false.

Screening A step in water treatment where water from lakes or rivers is passed through a series of wire meshes to remove floating debris such as plastic bags and branches.

Season A division of the year. It is marked by changes in the weather and by the number of daylight hours.

Secondary cell A cell that can be recharged.

Secondary colours When two primary colours combine, they produce the secondary colours yellow, cyan and magenta.

Sedimentary Rocks formed by layers of rock particles and dead plant and animal material building up over millions of years. Limestone and sandstone are examples of sedimentary rocks.

Seed A food store and protective coat that surrounds a plant embryo.

Seismology The study of volcanoes and earthquakes.

Semen The male reproductive fluid. It is made up of fluids from the seminal vesicles, prostate gland and Cowper's gland together with sperm.

Seminal vesicles Part of the male reproductive system. The seminal vesicles produce fluids that form semen, which nourish the sperm and allow them to swim.

Septum The heart is actually a double pump, separated into a left side and a right side by a central wall known as the septum.

Series When components in an electrical circuit are connected in line with each other and the battery, they are connected in series.

SETI (Search for Extra Terrestrial Intelligence) A project that involves listening with radio telescopes for radio signals emitted by other civilisations.

Settling A step in water treatment when the water flows into large tanks, where a chemical called aluminium sulfate is added. This helps small particles clump together and settle to the bottom of the tanks.

Sexual reproduction A form of reproduction that involves two parents. During fertilisation, male and female gametes fuse to form a zygote. The zygote divides to produce an individual.

Shadow Formed because light travels in straight lines and light cannot pass through opaque material.

Simple cell A cell that is made up of two different metals, called electrodes, placed in a chemical. This chemical can be in the form of a liquid or a paste.

SI units The accepted units of measurement for physical quantities.

Solar (energy) Solar cells generate electricity directly from sunlight.

Solar eclipse An event that happens when the Moon comes between the Sun and the Earth and causes a shadow to fall on the Earth's surface.

Solar system Our solar system includes the Sun and all the objects that orbit around it due to its gravity, including the Earth.

Solid When a substance is in the solid state, the particles that make up the substance touch because they are packed tightly together. The particles do not move around but they are not still, they vibrate on the spot.

Solubility A measure of how much solute can dissolve in a fixed volume of solvent to make a saturated solution.

Solubility curve A plot used to find out how soluble a particular solute is in a particular solvent at various temperatures.

Soluble Solids that dissolve are called soluble.

Solute The substance that dissolves in a solution.

Solution Formed when a solute dissolves in a solvent.

Solvent The substance that the solute dissolves into in a solution.

Sound (energy) A form of energy produced by vibrating waves.

Sound barrier It is possible to travel faster than sound in air. Doing so breaks the sound barrier.

Space Race The competition between Russia (formerly the USSR) and the USA about the use of rockets for space flight.

Space Shuttle Program The successor to the US Apollo programme. The Space Shuttle Program used reusable craft known as space shuttles.

Specialisation The adaptation of an organism or organ to carry out a special function.

Species A group of similar organisms that can breed with each other to produce fertile offspring.

Specimen A sample studied under a microscope.

Spectrum White light is made from seven combined colours, known as the spectrum of white light.

Speed The distance travelled per unit of time.

Speed of sound The speed of sound in air is around 330 m/s.

Sperm The male gamete in both plants and animals.

Spring balance A device that can be used to measure mass.

Stamen The male reproductive organs of flowering plants, made up of the anther and filament.

Star A ball of heat radiating gas that is held together by gravity. Stars contain mostly hydrogen as well as helium and smaller amounts of other elements.

Starvation When the food available to an individual organism or population does not meet their demand for energy or other key nutrients.

States of matter All matter exists in one of three states: solid, liquid and gas.

Static electricity When two objects come into contact, electrons can transfer between them. When this happens, both objects become charged with static electricity.

Stem A plant organ. A typical stem is a long above-ground rod. It is part of the shoot system, which develops from the plumule of a germinating seed.

Stigma A part of the female structure (carpel) in flowering plants. It acts as a landing area for a pollen grain which contains the male gamete (sperm).

Stimuli (singular: stimulus) All of the changes in an organism's environment.

Stomata Small pores on the underside of leaves through which gases pass into and out of the plant. Water vapour is also released through the stomata.

Stratosphere A layer of the Earth's atmosphere. The stratosphere ranges from 16 to 50 km above the Earth's surface and is 20 per cent of the atmosphere. The ozone layer is found in the stratosphere.

Streamlining Involves creating a smooth surface and an aerodynamic shape. Drag forces in wind and air can be reduced by streamlining.

Stretch When a material is stretched, the material's particles move further apart.

Style A part of the female structure (carpel) in flowering plants. The style is a stalk that positions the stigma for pollen collection.

Subatomic particles An atom is made up of even smaller particles called subatomic particles. Three subatomic particles are the proton, neutron and electron.

Sublimation A change of state from a solid to a gas without forming a liquid. The substance heated does not melt but turns directly into a gas.

Subscript The numbers to the lower right of a chemical symbol. They indicate the number of atoms of that element found in the compound

Substrate The substance an enzyme acts on. A substrate is equivalent to a reactant in a chemical reaction.

Sun The star that lights and heats our planet. The Sun is powered by a fusion reaction at its core.

Sunlight Energy flows to the Earth from the Sun in the form of sunlight, which is the source of energy used by producers such as plants to make their own food via photosynthesis.

Surface area A measure of how much of a substance is exposed.

Suspension If a solid does not dissolve it may either settle to the bottom of the liquid or end up floating throughout the liquid, making it cloudy. This is called suspension.

Sustainability Living in a way that meets the needs of our society without threatening the needs of future societies.

Symbiosis A relationship between organisms of different species where at least one benefits. The other organism may be unaffected, harmed or also benefit.

System A group of organs that work together to perform a task that an individual organ could not carry out on its own.

Systematic error This type of error causes all of the readings to be above or below the right value. Systematic errors normally happen when the measuring instrument is faulty or has not been set correctly, or when a person takes every measurement the wrong way.

Terrestrial planets Planets made up of rock. In our solar system, the terrestrial planets are the four inner planets.

Testes *(singular: testis)* A part of the male reproductive system. A male has two testes. The testes are located in the scrotum. The testes produce sperm (male gamete) and the male hormone testosterone.

Theory A hypothesis that has yet to be proven false.

Thermal *(energy)* Another term for heat energy.

Thermistor A device whose resistance decreases when it is heated.

Thermometer An instrument used to measure temperature.

Thermosphere A layer of the Earth's atmosphere. The thermosphere ranges from 80 to 640 km above the Earth's surface. The ionosphere and magnetosphere are also found here. This is the layer of the Earth's atmosphere that produces the aurora borealis.

Time A measurable period in which events or an event occurs.

Tissue A group of cells that work together to perform a particular task that an individual cell could not carry out on its own.

Titration An experimental technique used to find out exactly how much acid is needed to neutralise a base.

Total internal reflection A process by which light bounces through the glass of an optical fibre.

Traits Biologists often refer to characteristics as traits. For example, hair colour, accent and so on.

Translucent Translucent objects only allow some light to go through (not all), which forms a shadow that is very light. For example, a stained-glass window.

Transparent One of three ways that materials can be described in relation to light. Transparent objects allow light to pass through with no shadows formed. For example, a clear window.

Transpiration The loss of water vapour from the surface of a plant.

Tropism The directional growth response of a plant to a stimulus.

Troposphere A layer of the Earth's atmosphere. The troposphere ranges from 8 to 16 km above the Earth's surface and is 75 per cent of the atmosphere. This is where weather systems form.

Trough The lowest point of a wave.

Trundle wheel A piece of equipment that can be used to measure the length of long straight and curved lines.

Tumour A large mass of mutated cells.

Ultrasound A scan that uses high-frequency sound waves to create an image of the inside of the body.

Umbra The darkest part of the shadow during an eclipse. If you are standing in the umbra, the source of light is completely blocked by the object causing the shadow.

Unbalanced When one force on an object is stronger than another force, the forces are unbalanced. Unbalanced forces cause objects to speed up, slow down or change direction.

Unicellular Single cell. Bacteria and yeast are examples of unicellular organisms.

Universal indicator A mixture of dyes that change colour according to how concentrated an acid or alkali is. The advantage of universal indicator is that it shows the pH of the acid or alkali being tested.

Universe Everything that exists, including planets, stars, galaxies and all forms of matter and energy.

Upthrust The upward force exerted by a liquid. Pressure in liquids increases with depth, which means the bottom of something in a liquid will always feel more pressure than the sides because this point is the deepest.

Uranium A radioactive element. An isotope of the element uranium is used as a 'fuel' source for nuclear power.

Urethra A long tube located in the penis. During ejaculation, semen is transferred through the urethra to outside the body. Urine is also passed through the urethra from the bladder during urination (excretion).

Useful energy transfers Energy transfers that are wanted, such as the conversion of electricity to light in a light bulb.

Uterus A hollow organ with a strong muscular wall. Also called the womb. If a zygote is absent, then the lining of the womb is shed (menstruation). If pregnancy does occur, the uterus is the site of implantation, and the place where the embryo and foetus develops during pregnancy.

Vaccination The process of providing vaccines on a large scale.

Vaccine A treatment that protects the body from a particular disease. It is made from a weak or dead specimen of the pathogen that causes the disease.

Vacuoles

Vacuoles Membrane-bound cell structures that contain liquids. Animal cells contain small vacuoles. Plant cells often contain larger vacuoles full of water.

Vagina A part of the female reproductive system. The vagina is a muscular tube that receives the penis and semen during sexual intercourse. The sperm are deposited in the vagina. The vagina is also the passageway for menstruation and childbirth. It is sometimes called the birth canal.

Valency The combining power of an element. It is the number of bonds that an element needs to form a compound. For example, carbon has a valency of 4; it needs to form four bonds in a compound.

Variable A variable is any factor in an investigation that is able to change value. There are two types of variables: independent and dependent.

Variable resistor A device that can vary or change its resistance.

Variation All of the differences in traits that exist in members of the same species.

Vascular bundles The tissue responsible for transport in plants. There are two types of vascular tissue: xylem (transports water and minerals) and phloem (transports carbohydrates, usually in the form of sucrose). These bundles are very obvious as the veins on a leaf blade or on a freshly cut celery stem.

Vas deferens A part of the male reproductive system. The vas deferens is a tube that transfers sperm, as part of the semen, from the epididymis to the urethra during ejaculation. Also called the sperm duct.

Vector A physical quantity that has both magnitude and direction.

Vegetative propagation The artificial control of asexual reproduction in plants. Methods of vegetative propagation include cuttings, grafting and micropropagation.

Velocity Speed in a given direction. For example, 100 km/h south. Velocity of an object can be calculated by dividing the displacement of an object by the time taken to undergo that displacement.

Venae cavae *(singular: vena cava)* The major veins of the body. They carry deoxygenated blood, high in carbon dioxide, from all around the body to the right atrium of the heart.

Ventricles The two lower chambers of the heart.

Vernier calliper An instrument used for measuring widths, thicknesses and lengths of small objects.

Vertebrates Animals that do have a backbone.

Vibrate To produce sound, we need to make something vibrate.

Villi Finger-like projections that provide an increased surface area in the small intestine to allow the products of digestion to pass into the bloodstream.

Virus A small infectious agent with the ability to evolve and reproduce within a host cell. Viruses cause many diseases, including the common cold, influenza and Ebola.

Viscosity The flow rate of a liquid.

Vital signs Measures of a person's general health, such as temperature or heart rate.

Vitamins A biomolecule that is needed in small amounts to promote healthy gums, teeth, joints and immune system.

Voltage Potential difference in a circuit is also called voltage.

Voltmeter A device that can be used to measure voltage in a circuit.

Volts (v) The SI unit of potential difference (voltage).

Volume The volume of an object is the amount of space it takes up.

Waste (energy) Energy transfers that are not useful are known as wasteful.

Waste management The way that society deals with waste.

Waste minimisation A type of waste management that is often described as 'reduce, reuse, recycle'. It involves reducing waste at the source.

Water (H_2O) A key molecule for life. Water is an important part of cytoplasm and blood plasma. Water plays an important role in transport and temperature regulation. Water is also a key reactant in photosynthesis.

Water cycle Describes all of the changes that water undergoes as it moves through the Earth. The water cycle is powered by energy from the Sun.

Water treatment Describes the series of steps that water undergoes to make it fit for human use: screening, settling, filtration, chlorination and fluoridation.

Watt (W) The SI unit for power. The measure of how much energy is transferred per second in a machine is known as its power rating and is measured in watts.

Wave (energy) The movement of waves over large energy converting floats (e.g. a Pelamis) in the ocean can be used to generate electricity.

Wavelength The distance from the crest of one wave to the crest of another, measured in metres (m).

Wind

Wind *(energy)* A wind farm uses kinetic energy from the wind to turn turbines and generate electricity. Wind turbines spin generators to generate electricity.

Work What happens when an object is moved by a force.

World Wide Web (WWW) Allows us to use the internet to access and navigate between webpages using hyperlinks embedded on the pages.

X-rays High-energy electromagnetic waves that can pass through less dense tissue (e.g. muscles) but not through denser tissue (e.g. bone), making them useful for seeing the bones of the body.

Xylem A type of tissue in plants. Xylem tissue transports water and minerals up the plant stem from roots to leaves.

Zero error A type of systematic error. This happens when you use an instrument that has not been set to zero before use.

Zygote Forms when the sperm and egg fuse at fertilisation. The zygote develops into the embryo.